*unart*produktion

A Samurai on the Kriegerhorn

Legends for reading and hiking, by Daniela Egger
Illustrated by Daniel Nikolaus Kocher

Edition: May 2010
© unartproduktion Österreich
Mag. Ulrich Gabriel
6850 Dornbirn, Hatlerstraße 53
office@unartproduktion.at
www.unartproduktion.at
On behalf of: Lech Zürs Tourismus GmbH
www.lech-zuers.at
Text: Daniela Egger
Translation: Lingo24 www.lingo24.com
Illustrations: Daniel Nikolaus Kocher
Map: Copyright Land Vorarlberg –
Raumplanungsabteilung
Design: Werner Wohlgenannt
Cover design: Atelier Reinhard Gassner
ISBN 13: 978-3-901325-65-6 (deutsch)
ISBN 13: 978-3-901325-66-3 (italiano)
ISBN 13: 978-3-901325-67-0 (english)
ISBN 13: 978-3-901325-68-7 (français)

Happy reading and hiking!

Contents

Foreword 11

LECH – RÜFIKOPF – ZÜRS

Starting point: Lech [1] 17
A mysterious inheritance [2] 18
Wealth [3] 21
Rüfikopf [4] 23
The book [5] 25
Geological circuit [6] 27
Monzabonsee lake [7] 28
Alpe Monzabon [8] 30
Pazüelmähder [9] 32
Pazüelbach [10] 33
Trittalpe [11] 34
Hexenboden [12] 36
Watershed [13] 37
Zürs [14] 39

ZÜRS – ZUG

Hasenfluh [15] 43

The treasure in Zürsersee lake [16] 45

Taurin's cave [17] 46

The gate [18] 48

The glacial city of Madloch [19] 50

The bivouac [20] 52

Taurin on the Stierlochkopf mountain [21] 54

Farmer Jochum [22] 56

Gstütalpe [23] 57

Mining galleries [24] 58

Waterfall [25] 60

Zug [26] 61

ZUG – LECH

Scribbles [27] 65

Balmalp [28] 68

The monk and his Samurai [29] 69

Kriegeralpe [30] 73

Stone wall [31] 75

Gypsum holes [32] 77

Libellensee [33] 79

Omeshorn [34] 82

And back to Lech [35] 84

Acknowledgements and Biographies 88

Foreword

The Green Ring – a trail that takes "new paths"

Trails have a long tradition in the mountains. They provide the quickest and easiest route from one place to the next. They make landscapes accessible so they can be enjoyed and mapped. This changed with the advent of tourism, and especially with the discovery of the Alps for tourism. Trails were "made". Paths were created to allow mountain huts to be built and accessed. Trails to mountain peaks were forged so the mountains could be climbed. Pathways were carved out to important places.

The "Weisse Ring", or White Ring, is one of the most famous ski circuits and is considered by skiers to be one of the most legendary. It has been enthralling skiers from around the world for 50 years and has achieved almost cult status thanks to the White Ring ski race – an extraordinary skiing race with 1,000 participants who start the race en masse. However, the "Weisse Ring" also stands for speed and accessibility to the mountains.

The "Grüne Ring", or Green Ring, picks up on the concept of the white ring, builds on the idea and puts the emphasis back on nature. From time to time, you have to question traditions in order to be able continue them. You have to think about their function and content, as well as the values they represent. In this respect, it sometimes helps to take a look back at the past.

The "Grüne Ring" helps slow things down, sharpens your perception of the culture of this alpine environment, traces the relationships between people and tourism and provides the opportunity to view a famous landscape and enjoy the diversity of nature. While on the hike – which ideally should take three days – the area surrounding Lech und Zürs gradually reveals itself with each metre you climb up as well as each one you descend, and you begin to understand the nature of this landscape.

The "Grüne Ring" combines landscape and local legends in the form of an artistic concept that provides a breath of fresh air. Bregenz-based author Daniela Egger writes about historic legendary figures and the names of meadows, transporting them into a modern, global world and inventing new, wonderfully humorous legends about them. Stories from the past, as well as some from the future, make the landscape and the trails that cut through it come alive in a most unusual way and shed light predominantly on the invisible, the imaginable and the surprising.

Sculptor Daniel Nikolaus Kocher – whose involvement was, after that of Daniela Egger, the second stroke of luck for this project– has created a series of the installations along the route of the Green

Ring. These installations form a harmonious complement to the fairytale walks and masterfully perform a delicate balancing act between intrusion into a natural landscape and the staging of specially designed scenes at significant points along the route.

For me, the "Grüne Ring" is an exciting attempt to question the tried and tested, to rediscover cultural landscapes and tread "new trails". Thanks to a team of enthusiastic and creative people, the two artists mentioned, the active work of the community, the approval of the landowners, the help of the Skilifte ski lift company, the support of the hotels and restaurants, the Raiffeisenbank Lech and the local clubs and associations, this extraordinary hiking trail has been brought to life.

Josef Kyselak, an Austrian clerk and one of the most original writers of travel literature, famous for inscribing his name into the landscape while out hiking and therefore considered the father of graffiti, writes at the start of his book "Skizze einer Fussreise durch Österreich" [Sketches of a Journey on Foot through Austria]:

"God! There is only one world!
And anyone who doesn't like it,
Really should be here on earth
Nothing more than pity worth."

I hope you gain some unforgettable impressions on your walk around the Green Ring.

GERHARD WALTER, Lech Zürs Tourismus

LECH – RÜFIKOPF – ZÜRS

Starting point: Lech

Of course nowadays the people of Lech and Zürs are enlightened, modern people, business people and hospitality professionals who are in touch with the big wide world. If they remember their ancient legends and stories at all, they tend to relegate them to the realms of superstition and fantasy. However, closer research shows that the world of myth and its curious phenomena are not resting in the past, quite the opposite in fact – this supernatural world has overtaken the present and now comes back from the future to influence the activities of present-day life.. Its inhabitants are completely independent of time and place, and are therefore free. Since little attention is paid to them today, they have fun travelling through time and secretly asserting their influence.

A mysterious inheritance

So, for example a farmer's wife who had long since died, but was originally from Bürstegg flew into the future shortly after her death and saw how the small, insignificant place in the valley below had been completely transformed. The tourism business was booming and with it, the stock markets. In order to leave her offspring something really valuable, she bought shares and funds in the bank in Lech, which she put in her will in the past. The papers were stamped with the date on which the bequest was made. She trusted that her two daughters would be smart enough to keep the papers, even if they did not understand what they were. Ninety years later, a granddaughter of this woman found the papers in her mother's estate and took them to the bank to have them valued. To this day, the bank staff continue to rack their brains as to how they should estimate the value of these mysterious, but entirely genuine papers and, more importantly, what would happen if the owners wanted to cash in the papers. Not only would they own the bank and all its assets at one fell swoop, they would also own half of the East. Fortunately, the famous bank crash came shortly thereafter and the woman never mentioned the papers again.

Wealth

In the past, many knew of the resident household spirits, but nobody really knew whether they were friendly or malicious. Unable to trust them, people would try to banish them to another place. Nowadays, our relationship with them has changed: we do not acknowledge them and nobody wants to say they have seen one - for the time being at least. However, behind some rather mundane doors, all manner of resources are being used to bring back spirits that were once banished, because they have proved to be lucrative after all, even if not necessarily friendly. Bringing them back has its own problems though because these beings are stubborn and, as shape-shifters, can remain undetected. Today, if a black poodle pops up somewhere, it could be the Monzabon spirit having fun while causing confusion in the form of an ancient Lech spirit. Since in public nobody would admit to the suspicion that a poodle is anything more than just a poodle, these lively creatures sneakily manage to cause quite a stir – after all, that is their main job. A sure sign that a real spirit has returned to its place of origin is the sudden wealth that breaks out in the area. But you just keep quiet about the changes because spirits are extremely secretive and there is no need to draw attention to them.

Rüfikopf

The rugged summit of this mountain towers above the small village of Lech and here begins not just the hike around the Green Ring, but the history of Lech and Zürs. The Rüfikopf is in fact the real reason why this little village came into being. Resentful, it watches over every little geological change that occurs. And it needs to because in its ridge lurk tectonic forces which, as the mountain unfolded, were far from finished when the Rüfikopf thought in its stubborn head that the valley before it should remain as it was. The plates beneath it keep on pressing and pushing incessantly in an effort to ultimately unfold the little valley bottom too as intended and continue their work. But the Rüfikopf found a kind of dance, a rhythmic movement deep within itself. This is how it absorbs the pressure from below. Eventually, a melody developed to go with the dance; a fast, driving rhythm that can be most closely compared with rap. Deep within its rocky interior, the Rüfikopf raps and moves to the rhythm and hence it is fully able to neutralise these tectonic forces. This has all been going on for a very, very long time. And this is how the mountain became the real custodian of the geological profile of the region, and Taurin, a sensitive, roaming giant, understood what was happening before him because he could hear the ancient rapping within the mountain. And Taurin decided to help the Rüfikopf, but that's another story.

The book

It is not as easy as it sounds. Of course, there are summit books in other places and they are well known. You climb a mountain and when you are right at the top, on the summit, you enter you name and the date in the summit book – and your successful ascent is recorded. The Rüfikopf also has such a book, as do both of the other summits along the Green Ring – the two counterparts of this book can be found on Kriegerhorn and on Madlochsattel. Externally, they differ very little from other samples of this type – but they only purport to be simple summit books. In fact, nobody can recall ever having put them there – how they got there remains a mystery. And as for their true purpose, well the only information available is sketchy and creates a curious picture. We know that the three books are connected and possibly communicate in a way that we do not understand. They swap names and dates with each other. What we also know is that some names disappear from the pages without a trace while other names transfer to both the other books although the hikers involved have never hiked the entire trail. Hence, their names could not have been entered at

Kriegerhorn, for example, or at Madlochsattel. Somehow, the three books provide a unique list of names that is constantly expanding and at certain times of the year, they match each other exactly – although the people who have entered themselves in the list have not hiked all of the three summits. We also now know that these names all belong to people who have one thing in common: they are influential and good people in their own way. They are people who do their work with peaceful intentions and do good either in private or in public (there's a big difference). The fact that the list keeps changing by itself has prompted some people to check again after a year to see whether their names are still in the book. It is rumoured that there are people who suddenly turned their life around – they initiated environmental protection projects or financed schools in Africa, or at least became vegetarian, simply because their name had disappeared from the book. Should you decide to make the effort and climb one of these three peaks, you should probably think carefully about entering your name in a summit book – it could have far-reaching consequences for your lifestyle.

Geological circuit

Taurin, the giant, was passing through with his sister when they both came to the Rüfikopf mountain and heard the rock rapping. Taurin then returned to the Stierlochkopf mountain region to record his work. While his sister waited for him to come back, she passed the time making a mosaic out of the shells and snails they had collected on their travels across many countries. She liked the pattern so much that in the end she decided to push the pretty little creatures deep into the rock of the Rüfikopf mountain and then she sanded them down with her rough hands so they would remain clearly visible before heading off to follow her relatives to Albania. There have been numerous geological investigations and there are currently some audacious theories that the ancient ocean reached this altitude and the shells, snails and fish were natural deposits – but that is all wrong.

Monzabonsee lake

For a long time, there has been a spirit living in the lake close to the woody mountain who enjoys singing. Because she sings in different registers and always sings the name of her homeland, mont salvanu, from underwater, people gradually understood what the place should be called. Most people heard her, but the words were unclear and muffled by the water so they returned to the valley with a wide variety of interpretations. It is, therefore, not surprising that many different spellings have prevailed, including Montzabon, Munzabun, Munzenbun, Montapan, Montapon and Montzapon. They all sound beautiful when sung and it is recommended that you sing them joyously at the top of your voice when you are close to the lake because it is said that the spirit is waiting for a reply and will award a pot of gold for the most beautiful voice.

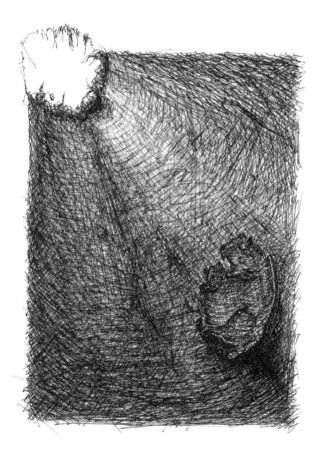

Alpe Monzabon

Buramänta is what the locals call those most curious of animals, the marmots. Many of them have settled on the slopes of Alpe Monzabon to conduct important research – their job is to observe people at high altitudes. Often you will see them, amazed at the blindness of the hikers and herdsmen, who, careless and ignorant, pass by the most dazzling apparitions of the supernatural world. They shake their heads in disbelief at the naivety with which the simple confront very powerful beings and believe they are not being watched. Of all things, they then decide to throw away their rubbish or take off their clammy hiking boots to dip their not exactly fresh feet into the cool water right in front of an already evil-eyed water witch – unsuspecting of whose company they are keeping, practically everywhere. Of course, it is rare that anything worth mentioning happens because most of these beings are patient and find their visitors at most annoying. Only a few people overstep the mark and then something does happen, which is later passed off as a harmless accident or put down to the person's own clumsiness or just described as "a bit strange". The Buramänta then disappear, whining, into their branched tunnel system to make a report – they are not allowed to intervene, that has always been forbidden for research troops because it would distort the outcome of the investigations. However, sometimes they can barely tolerate it and flee, wailing, into the depths – or they remain transfixed and stand not quite hidden behind the hill, keeping track of every detail. When that happens, people find it charming that the cute marmots are showing such an interest in them – then they accidentally go and stand on the foot of the next hobgoblin.

Pazüelmähder

Pazüelmähder is an area not inhabited by the supernatural, it belongs entirely to the enlightened spirit of the 21st century. This could be down to the clear waters that spring up along the gentle slopes of the meadows and flow into the Pazüelbach stream. Even the name Pazüel is suggestive of an ancient water source: puteolu – a spring – must have been hiding somewhere in the meadows. Here, it is only natural that the old wooden huts by the side of the trail are filled with books, the representatives of intellect and enlightenment. They invite you to stop for a while, be inspired and relax – far from any sinister and unsavoury society. Here, everything is in full view, there are no strange noises, no supernatural thoughts being conveyed over the rolling hills. It is a place of tranquillity, until later, deep below, it becomes eerie again.

Pazüelbach

The Pazüelbach stream continues downwards, flowing over a steep cliff into the depths. Waterfalls have forever been stomping grounds for all the VIPs of the supernatural world. Here, with a little luck, the hiker will be offered a rare opportunity. Falling water, if you stare at it long enough, reflects your own state of mind. It reveals many an awful vision of greed, contempt or misery and the features of this vision often bear a striking resemblance to the observer. These ghosts are attached to the person by umbilical cords and they constantly whisper the name of their creator. This is a useful tip because if you know that most frightful forms arise from one's own emotional state, then you have the key to liberate yourself. But the simple fact is, not everybody wants to get rid of their howling company – in truth, hardly anybody takes the time to stare long enough into the mirror-like water to be able to recognise themselves in it. Instead, you can stroll along the narrow trail without a care in the world and just enjoy the sound of the water.

Trittalpe

Close to Trittalpe hides something special that even today still excites souls on both sides. Neither the creatures of the supernatural world nor the people who find the mystical path can offer a logical explanation. In certain weather conditions, this mystical path sometimes branches off from the hiking route and leads quite naturally and directly to a rock, at which point it ends abruptly. What is hiding behind the rock, nobody knows – the people of the night, however, speculate that Taurin the giant made a mistake here at some point. They whisper, amused that Taurin wanted to bring a heavy boulder back to the Stierlochkopf mountain and then, realising it didn't belong there, simply dropped it – in the middle of a trail. But Taurin remains stubbornly silent and does not want to help clarify this issue.

However, one of the magicians from ancient times became deeply engrossed in another theory and remains to this day petrified with anger in front of the rock gate that he could not open with any of his spells.

Hexenboden

Hexenboden could be translated as "witches' ground" and a place with a name like this must have earned it somehow! It was here that a ski lift operator finally tried to put an end to all the chaos the famous witches brought and obstructed their established dancing area with a chairlift system. Unfortunately, this didn't bother the modern witches in the slightest. Quite the opposite in fact: where previously they had to struggle with uncomfortable broomsticks, now they could use the nice comfy seats that were already up there. Not much is needed from the old art of magic to twirl these seats merrily through the air. The witches' dance has since become an even bigger attraction, enticing visitors from all over the world. The same trend can be seen in the small village down in the valley where rather colourfully dressed and happily nonconformist women with foreign accents are no longer a rarity.

Watershed

Long ago, the watershed at Flexenpass used to be a popular playground for the witches. Here, witches were able to upset the natural balance of water distribution with ease. A quick spell cast on the left-hand side and the majority of the melting snow would flow into the Black Sea. The North Sea would begin emptying until one of the witches from the North came to Lech to break or, as was more often the case, reverse the spell. Then, the water level in the Black Sea would fall and the North Sea would be crashing with renewed vigour against the cliffs and dykes. When it reached the point where there wasn't enough water in the Black Sea for a proper storm, one of the witches in Constanza would think it had gone too far and would race to Flexenpass to manipulate the watershed. And so the game went on, round and round in circles until the people of Lech became really fed up with it. It wasn't the differences in water levels in distant countries that annoyed them, but the bad-tempered witches who regularly turned up in the village and tampered with Flexenpass – because they were an incalculable risk for tourism. So, the locals decided to build an installation which for some time now has allowed hikers to redirect the water by hand. If you scoop the water to the right, it flows into the Black Sea and if you scoop to the left, it flows into the North Sea. It being so easy to change the water direction now means it has become too hectic for the witches to keep interfering as well, plus they have to make a long and uncomfortable journey to get there in the first place. So, Flexenpass is now a peaceful place and the wild women only meet to party in Hexenboden – and there they are usually in a good mood!

Zürs

Cyclones do not really feature heavily in our country. Their creators usually inhabit the horizon over the Caribbean and the USA – but when the clans are arguing and getting on top of each other, a family member may be sent far away to a distant country. One of these very powerful clan lords has been living in Zürs for a little while. In human years, it seems as if his stay is lasting an eternity, but it is always a question of life expectancy and line of perception. In any case, this descendant of a powerful family is under strict instructions to keep quiet and avoid attracting attention: the more eddies he causes in Pfurra and around Zürs, the longer he must remain in exile. He has successfully managed to obey his instructions, apart from the odd incident such as where a whole herd has flown over a fence or a man, together with his daughter, has been swept along from Zürs to Lech, it is relatively quiet. Still, the people of Zürs would be happy if this particular guest would go away soon, for good, because things he and his kind do not consider worth mentioning, they consider major disturbances. Should a tourist ever be lost in a cyclone created by them, the region would suffer a crisis of image – but plans for this kind of emergency have already been drawn up and are kept under lock and key in the Tourist Office.

ZÜRS – ZUG

Hasenfluh

Ignaz died while using a double sleigh to bring wood to the valley. What happened? The rear sleigh tipped over and broke his leg. It was already late in the evening. Ignaz could do nothing more than crawl on his belly towards the valley, but at some point he fell still and died from the cold and exhaustion. He froze to death without realising it because when he woke up it was still night time and the middle of winter, but he felt light-footed and relaxed like he hadn't been in a long time. Only, he could not move the stupid sleigh with the wood, despite trying for ages to turn it back the right way up. At some point, the snow melted, the summer came and went, the sleigh remained rigid and immovable and Ignaz waited for help or tried to force the bulky thing over. Sometimes, hikers would pass by, their clothes increasingly peculiar and their faces increasingly foreign. Ignaz could not comprehend it all, but when he tried to get one of them to finally help him with this problem, he noticed that he could sink into their body without resistance. He could calmly discern the stranger's thoughts and mull them over and his own thoughts were able to flow effortlessly into strangers' minds. He enjoyed this so much, he whiled away decades doing it. He learned a lot from the strangers' thoughts. Some clever hikers had passed by, and some not so clever. Over time, Ignaz became a really good judge of character. He suspected that quite a lot of time must have passed since his fall because the snow had stopped and started again many times, melting away and then coming back. But Ignaz had stopped thinking about time because it had become unimportant to him. He is now an educated man and shares his knowledge with strangers by passing new thoughts into their minds whenever he has nothing better to do.

The treasure in Zürsersee lake

"The treasure in Zürsersee lake" was a famous TV show about 50 years ago that attracted hordes of hikers to Zürs seeking adventure. There was a veritable gold rush because lots of visitors believed the story was true and came armed with all sorts of tools to dig for the legendary treasure in and around the lake. The ski lift companies made the most of the gold diggers' enthusiasm to dig by spreading strategic rumours about where it would be best to dig next – hence a wide path was created quickly and cost-effectively around the lake! The one-time gold diggers had also built a floating platform on the water's surface to make it easier to dig in the depths of the lake. Today, the picturesque wooden platform serves as an ideal rest area in a place that was once all hustle and bustle, but now offers peace and tranquillity. Only the ski lift companies continue to dig and build, less in the search for treasure buried somewhere deep and more out of a passion for construction per se.

Taurin's cave

From the platform, you have a direct view of a cave that is at the centre of another legend associated with treasure. Legend has it that Taurin the giant retreats into this cave when he takes his long sleep in the winter. During the summer, he only comes by now and again to check his belongings are still there. He is only really passing through. After completing his self-imposed task relating to the Stierlochkopf mountain, he intends to continue travelling and because he needs to put his luggage somewhere, he puts it in the cave. To deter the curious from going too far into the cave, he has built all sorts of terrifying obstacles, most of which, however, are imperceptible to humans because they are intended for a much more dangerous nuisance to Taurin – the little goblins that live in the cotton grass meadow nearby. The goblins discovered the value of his possessions long ago and wanted to steal them from him. However, no people have ever seen them, except perhaps for one man who apparently once entered the cave seeking shelter from a storm – but no one knows that for sure. When he emerged some days later from the dark cave, which was filled with nooks and crannies, he was mute, completely grey and he died just a few weeks later without ever being able to tell anyone what had happened in there.

The gate

The trail continues on to a small hill, behind which there is a large, enchanting cotton grass field. Depending on the weather, pretty streams trickle through the ancient glacial basin. As idyllic as this place may seem, it is inhabited by small, but very powerful beings that are not to be messed with. They prefer passers-by to be unobtrusive and not hang around for too long. It therefore makes good sense to approach the field in a stooping posture. The best approach is the disused tunnel that was built a long time ago – though nobody knows why or by whom. The goblins do not just inhabit this meadow, they have built an intricate system of underground tunnels and move, completely unhindered by the force of gravity and others laws of nature, on the surface or beneath it – or even half inside and half outside the ground. They also like to fly around in the air, but they are so quick and agile that practically no one has spotted them. They imitate animal sounds or familiar bird calls, then laugh at the hikers' searching looks as they scan the area trying to find the animals. Despite all these practical jokes, we should not forget that these little guys can be very unfriendly, especially if you get too close to them. They are always busy with very important, top secret matters so move along quickly and at the most steal a quick glance at the mysterious gate which a long time ago marked the boundary of the ancient glacial city.

The glacial city of Madloch

The cotton grass meadow sits picturesquely in front of the slip rock slopes of the ancient glacial foothills. As the majestic glacier pushed its icy tip into the sky, the entrance to a now buried city could be found on this foothill. Its inhabitants had created a truly advanced civilisation and a peaceful society by freeing themselves of earthly needs through absolute asceticism and meditation. When they were ready to live without food and warmth, even in inhospitable ice caves, they retreated into the depths of the glacier and built a magnificent city of ice and light. Unimpeded by greed and the need for survival, they lived in a hidden world, acting as guardian spirits for the people nearby. But nature had other plans, the glacier melted and the city was buried within as its slopes gave way. The snowy beings began searching for a new place to live and wandered, so the story goes, as far as Tibet. Not long after that, the roof of the world became known as a bastion of peace in the midst of war and hardship. Even the meditation techniques that are now gradually returning from the East to the West are products of the civilisation that originated in Madloch. But that was all a long time ago – only remnants of the magnificent glacial city can still be seen glistening from within the rock on bright days.

The bivouac

At the foot of the Stierlochkopf mountain stands a modern bivouac made from wood, installed by mountain rescue to provide a safe place to stay during bad weather. In many ways, it is a breathtaking place to sleep. The panoramic views alone that you can enjoy before you go to sleep warrant this claim. But unfortunately, the night could turn out to be a breathtaking experience should it by chance be one of those rare "silver nights". On these nights, the poor, exploited miners who once dug for silver and bronze in this area commemorate their former, forfeited lives. They were considered lazy and slovenly, which they probably were to some extent. On silver nights, however, they are driven by an ambition they never experienced during their lifetime: since they dwell in the supernatural world, they are able to detect even the finest slither of silver hiding within the mountain with the naked eye. They dig so zealously and noisily into the depths that not only does the mountain shake (and with it, the bivouac), but Taurin also emerges from his hiding place, cursing and trying to drive away the intruders. Now, these nights are extremely rare so the probability of getting caught up in a dispute between Taurin and his enemies, the miners, is a remote one – but unfortunately these nights are not marked on any calendar available to us humans. An overnight stay in the bivouac is definitely worthwhile, but if all around starts to shake and there is uproar outside, stay inside the hut and try not to draw attention to yourself.

Taurin on the Stierlochkopf mountain

It is an incredibly laborious task that this poor guy took upon himself. For the mountain does what mountains always do: move, fold up, throw off rocks, shed their outer layer, stretch out. And Taurin the giant was appalled by this. He thought the mountain was perfect as it was when he first saw it and made it his job to return it to its former shape. No one could dissuade him – Taurin was compelled to see Stierlochkopf back in its ideal shape. Legend has it that the mountain shook several times, huge boulders falling to the ground, and each time Taurin burst into tears and promised the summit that he would bring all the rocks back up. Stierlochkopf was not really bothered because its mind had been on other things for a long time – and when the time was right, it shook briefly and all the superfluous rocks rolled off it like scales peeling off skin. Nevertheless, Taurin has been busy carrying the heavy boulders back up and neatly piling them back on top ever since.

Farmer Jochum

This is also why Farmer Jochum once tried in vain to build a chapel on his land. As coincidence would have it, he loaded his donkey with a selection of nice-shaped stones from the Stierlochkopf mountain, intending to use them for the planned building works. Throughout the day, he worked on the wall whenever he got the chance. The next morning, the stones had been thoroughly dismantled. Farmer Jochum did not know how thorough Taurin was; in fact, he had no idea Taurin even existed. But Taurin now knew the farmer and he was sorry that he had to undo his work every night – but it didn't help because he was convinced that every last one of the Stierloch stones had to be returned to its rightful place. Otherwise his work would never be done and he would have to remain in Lech for ever, all the while yearning to be in faraway Albania with his relatives.

Gstütalpe

For a long time, it was thought that this name referred to a place where a rare breed of horse was bred that would be particularly suited to working at these high altitudes. But now the theory is that the name Gstüt just refers to the old word "Stude", which means a bush or shrub. So the famous Przewalski horses come from the mountain valleys of Tachin Schara Nuru and not from the precursors to the Alps. But that doesn't matter; the area around the Gstütalpe still has plenty of special features to offer. One famous horse more or less makes no difference.

Mining galleries

Knappenlöcher, or "Chnappalöcher", as they are actually called, are mining galleries. They are the remnants of a time long ago when wages were so very meagre that even the scant earnings to be had from mining for silver, calamine and zinc blende seemed worthwhile. The work was hard, the mining areas remote and the supervision sporadic. So the young chaps who were supposed to be doing the mining often spent their days dozing on the sunny slopes, sometimes drunk. They knew how dangerous it was to be crawling into the deep shafts when they were drunk, ineptly digging for the coveted metal with unsuitable tools. The number of accidents there had been already meant this dangerous job was not exactly desirable. Hence, more often than he would have liked, the guardian of the castle had to check that everything was in order. Already cursing, he would set off from the Gstütalpe, where presumably the charcoal kilns were kept, on his way to the mining galleries to unleash his tirade. But the young miners received warning of his approach because the wind carried his cursing over the slopes and so they would disappear, drunk or sober, inside the tunnels in good time before the angry patron even came into sight. Unfortunately, one day whilst hurriedly trying to scramble into the tunnel, two of the young men slipped and broke a beam they had grabbed in an attempt to halt their fall. With the support beam broken, the tunnel came crashing down on the two men. Their bodies were later recovered and buried in white shrouds. Since then, they have on occasion been seen clambering out of the tunnel. As they think they have not been seen, they chat away merrily and seem quite happy. They wear their white burial attire, which is still clean, and they move with incredible agility, heading in whatever direction their thoughts might take them. Only when they realise they are being watched do they start their horrendous whining in order to present an image of unlucky victims buried alive.

Waterfall

The waterfall on the opposite river bank from Zug can, with a little luck, provide the backdrop to a very rare sight for hikers. The springy stone pools bubbling with glacial waters are a popular bathing place of the mysterious women of Heuberg, a little known and timid race of people who live in secrecy and are still very much in touch with nature and its laws. They are easily several hundred years old, yet exceptionally beautiful. However, they have another quality which is particularly rare nowadays: they are joyful and exuberant. It is rumoured that they live in caves, eat roots and medicinal plants and love music. They are not inhabitants of the supernatural world though, quite the opposite: you could say they are far more lively and "of this earth" than some people alive today! What distinguishes them from us can be summed up in one word: happiness. Sometimes they even appear at dance festivals and party and sing along playfully, but eventually they disappear back into the night.

Zug

The fact that the small village of Zug sits directly en route to the area where the people of the night go to dance may have often tormented the poor villagers. One time, however, these people of the night were in high spirits and, feeling friendly, they stopped at a farmer's and lit a bonfire in front of his cowshed. To his horror, they led his best cow out of the shed and slaughtered it, carefully removed its hide and cooked some wonderful joints of meat – a feast that the strange beings shared with the poor farmer's children who had never had full bellies before in their lives, let alone eaten anything that tasted so delicious. However, the people of the night insisted that none of the cow's bones be broken or lost. The farmer wailed and complained. Losing his best cow was a great misfortune and he did not know how he would survive the harsh winter now. The people of the night just laughed and played and danced and partied the whole night long. Before they disappeared into the dawn, they gathered up all the bones. One was missing and they all searched fervently for it. Eventually, the sun was about to rise over the mountain crest and the people of the night became frantic

– they sighed that the cow would just have to be left with a limp and hurriedly wrapped the bones in the hide. Then they disappeared. The next minute, the cow was standing in its shed and, for the rest of its life, dragged one leg behind it.

ZUG – LECH

Scribbles

The night people of Zug tend to gather at the waterfall, initially to invoke the special forces that exist in such places. They are an uninhibited group of hedonistic beings from a different world – what unites them is their desire to party. All of them bring intoxicating substances and try each other's secret substances, which often leads to odd and even regrettable excesses. Their actual end destination though is usually the Balmalp because there is a secluded ledge there that is big enough for a gathering of partygoers to dance and, it has to be said, even copulate on. The route leads them back to Zug and through the village and then zigzags through the forest. The people of Zug are used to it and close their shutters and doors at night, hoping that the procession of night people will pass by without disturbing them. That's the way it has been for generations. What has been reported about the people of the night is, unfortunately, not for the ears of children. However, there is something childlike about them because on their way through the forest, generations of night people, including children, have left markings and scribbles on tree trunks and rootstalks. You

might think that they must have already been in-
toxicated and not quite with it, but, given the curious
symbols and figures carved in the wood, you have to
marvel at the childish nature of these otherwise not
exactly demure hooligans.

Balmalp

What exactly has gone on in the naturally secluded area beneath the rock, i.e. beneath the Balme, nobody wants to know. But it has become a popular place to party. A warm lounge along with a pretty observation terrace have now been built here - to the immense delight of the night people since they too are fond of modern architecture and appreciate the comfort of timber floors and wooden benches with a nice view.

The monk and his Samurai

Where the names Kriegerhorn and Kriegeralpe come from in an area that has no tradition of war whatsoever is a mystery because "Krieger" means "warrior". What's more surprising is that the word is also used for a certain type of cart that was designed for transporting topsoil and manure. This type of cart is also used in wood clearing activities. However, what's much, much more astonishing is the use of this old word for the medicinal herb arnica – in many places, this plant is called a "Krieger" (warrior). It is no longer possible to determine why the name Kriegeralpe was chosen, but maybe research into this question has overlooked something important – it is rumoured that a monk, who came from distant Japan to explore the Alps, actually climbed the Kriegerhorn. The monk was accompanied by a Samurai who was in full armour. The poor warrior struggled up to the summit, sweating, behind the lightly clad monk. The warrior had been ordered by the emperor of his kingdom to protect the monk and he took his job very seriously. He patiently followed the monk through valleys, over mountain slopes and up to the summit. The monk was looking for remnants of an ancient civilisation featured in a Japanese legend. The legend apparently has its origins in the Alps or in their foothills and tells of a strangely peaceful people who had once retreated into the glacier. These people, for reasons we do not know, later moved to the East and once they arrived in faraway Tibet, an advanced, spiritual civilisation blossomed there, which many hundreds of years later also reached Japan. The monk wanted to bring back evidence to Japan that would prove the story was true so persuaded the emperor to finance the study trip. The Samurai accompanied the monk for many years and observed with concern that the monk was increasingly losing hope in his ideas and was becoming more and more confused: he mumbled incoherently, appeared to be seeing things and pursued every crazy little idea. After many years of searching without any hint of success, the Samurai had grown weary of it all. He no longer believed there was any truth in the ancient legend and eventually he even thought the man he had been ordered to protect had lost his mind. And right on the Kriegerhorn, after scouring the 120 peaks of the eastern Alps and with the whole of the western Alps stretching out, unexplored, before them, the warrior had finally had enough. He drew his sword and cut the monk's head off. Peace at last. Afterwards, he killed himself in the traditional Samurai fashion. Since neither monk nor Samurai haunted the area, this story was soon forgotten, but perhaps the name Kriegerhorn is intended to remind us of it.

71

Kriegeralpe

Officially, the reservoir was built to ensure there was sufficient water in the winter for the thirsty snow cannons. Unofficially, however, there is another reason for its existence: the lake was formed when a comet hit. It blew a deep crater into the bedrock, rain broke out immediately and filled the hole with water, creating an ideal home for the guest that the comet had brought with it. It seems it was a being from an advanced civilisation that likes to stay hidden beneath the water. We don't know much about it, but we do know one thing for sure: it is trying make contact with humans. Every now and then it makes symbols and figures on the water's surface that reveal surprisingly banal messages. We assume that it is trying to work out if there is intelligence in the area. However, it isn't making much progress with these attempts at contact, maybe because it seems to be away for long periods of time. Sometimes, the lake lights up like a star at night and then the water disappears and the crater bulges outwards. The research team based at the bottom of the Kriegerhorn that was set up to document these mysterious events doesn't know exactly what is going on. They don't like to talk about what they have seen.

Stone wall

For once, there is a phenomenon on the Green Ring that may have a plausible explanation: the stone wall in Oberlech, where the names of all the residents of Lech and Zürs have been recorded since 2010. People bring pebbles with their names and dates of birth etched into them and a skilled craftsman stacks them to form a wall. There's nothing mysterious about it, it's just a clever and quaint idea. And in a couple of centuries, when electronic data has disintegrated into a pixel salad for ever more and paper can only be read under an airtight glass cover, this wall will be quite long and the names of the proud locals will remain intact come wind, rain or snow. Should subsequent civilisations ever carry out excavation work in the area, it may well be that the people of the distant future find little other than these names – impressive evidence of a small yet indomitable people with foresight.

Gypsum holes

Long ago, there was an old road leading from Mittelberg to Hochkrumbach and from there over the Geißbühel hill and past the gypsum holes; it continued over the Tannberg mountain and Zug leading down into the Walsertal valley and from there on to Feldkirch. It is perhaps because of this old road that strange phenomena occur every now and then in and around the gypsum holes in the Berger Alpe mountains. Sometimes you can hear peculiar cries of joy coming from the holes – and if a brave shepherd or hiker cries back, it suddenly sounds like they are so close that, to date, everyone has just ran away as fast as they can. Also, two chaps all dressed in white keep being seen emerging from the holes where gravity appears to have no effect: the men barely move their legs and yet still leap in no time at all from the funnel-shaped recesses over the Schneckenrain on to the Tannberg fields, a steep area where farmers used to wear crampons for mowing. Of course, the crumbly gypsum karst of this area lends itself to underground tunnels and caves, but why these two men went underground there and what they do when they come out onto the surface, nobody knows to this date. But that's no surprise because this secret will only be revealed in the distant future from whence these two figures appear every now and then. Where they enter and leave will be their future workplace (the shopping centre which will extend deep into the gypsum karst and which has something very special to offer that cannot be revealed right here and now). The strange white garments they wear are said to reflect the fashion of the time. Their astonishing speed is based on a new transportation technology that will finally put an end to noisy cars. But all that is a long time off yet. The fact that these events happen along an old road that has long since disappeared is no coincidence – people and other beings are always drawn to places where there once used to be a road.

Libellensee

In the 1930s, a small, hidden lake would tempt guests of the former "Hohe Welt" hotel to slip in for a swim or just to relax. Back then there was already a narrow boardwalk that led around the lake and deep into the dark forest. The hotel owner completely removed the section that led into the forest using construction equipment, but the next day it was all back in place. Even prohibition signs and wood clearing activities didn't achieve the desired result – no matter what he tried, the next day everything would be back to how it was the day before. However, just as the boardwalk reappeared every day, unfortunately guests disappeared every day into the depths of the forest, so eventually the lake had to be abandoned. When that happened, the guests stopped coming and the hotel fell empty. But what today sounds like a harmless stroll through the cool shade of the woods was back then a big attraction – lots of guests, many of them famous, only came to Oberlech for that reason. Anyone who returned from the woods had changed radically. To be more precise, the guests came back from the woods looking some years younger and many of them emphasized the effects by using rejuvenating treatments while others played it down – in any case, a lot of them had difficulties with their passports when trying to cross the international borders to get home and had to get new IDs. The hotel owner pleaded with the guests, who arrived in their hordes, to take a walk in the fresh mountain air and trust in the beneficial effects of exercise and healthy eating instead. But that wasn't what they had come to his hotel for. At some point, the owner decided he had had enough of this business and took a long holiday himself. He left the bathing lake and boardwalk to be overgrown. Rumour has it that he made up the holiday and had in fact vanished into the woods himself for a long time. Today, the bathing lake is well looked after again, but long walks in the forest do not have the same effect the whole world was talking about back then.

Escalator

This lake is probably one of the most magical places on the Green Ring. While walks in the forest seem to have lost their rejuvenating effect, to replace it, the boardwalk has developed a life of its own. For some time now, it seems to have been digging itself into the ground and sometimes, you can hear its wooden slats rattling as if it were an escalator burrowing into the depths. We don't know exactly what is going on in the earth's interior there, but we do know one thing for sure: for a while, strange air bubbles have been seen rising from the depths of the lake and, for some unknown reason, suddenly there is a pump next to the boardwalk. Visitors are urged not to touch it for whenever anyone touches it, new and powerful bubbles are generated that emit a mysterious gas. Investigations have concluded that, if inhaled, this gas causes immediate and complete cell regeneration. However, the long term effects of this have not yet been studied. It is rumoured that this installation is part of some secret research station. Nobody knows who put it there or on whom research is being conducted – well it's probably the naïve hiker who is curious enough to activate the pump and inhale the gas. But, until all this is fully clarified, we would ask that you be sensible and avoid the lake altogether. Trust in the beneficial effects of exercise in the fresh air and healthy eating, and forget all about the mysterious rejuvenating effects of the Libellensee lake.

Omeshorn

In the silhouette and under the protection of this mountain lie the villages of Lech, Zürs and Zug, as well as the entire hiking circuit of the Green Ring. The Omeshorn has to be the most important phenomenon in this magical place. Calmly and quietly it sits in the middle of the villages, motionless to the human eye, but don't be fooled by its stillness. Mountains, rivers and valleys are of course themselves living things too. They are a different kind of living thing, but nevertheless they communicate and perform their duties selflessly. They don't make a fuss like some of the elemental beings we have talked about (which are good for rumours and legends) and they don't want to be gossiped about all the time. However, one story does have to be told – the one about the pretty will-o'-the-wisp on the Omeshorn which is often believed to be a spirit and is feared, but in reality, it is a sign of the friendliness of the mountain: it hates it when people get lost in the dark and can't find their way home; it detests seeing people wandering around in despair. The solution is simple, if you ask the mountain for light, it will light up your way home for you. Only humans have still not learned to return to their friends and family gratefully and silent; instead they arrive home and make a lot of fuss about the mysterious spirit on Omeshorn mountain. But the mountain doesn't get angry, it remains silent – and will always be there to provide light again when it is needed.

And back to Lech

The period between 1850 and 1900 was known as the Little Ice Age. Back then the village was so cut off that the majority of its inhabitants moved down to the countryside to find work. Only 300 people stayed in Lech. Construction of the new road was crucial for the survival and the economic growth of this village, but that is another story. Right now, we want to tell you about an old prophecy concerning the church in Lech. It has been foretold that foxes will one day jump in and out of the sound holes of its bell tower, when the glacier stretches far into the valley once more and the Tannberg is covered with ice. At that time, the world will allow itself another little rest, leave the manic fever of capitalism behind it and curb the fervour of its inhabitants. Even though from today's perspective a new Little Ice Age may seem undesirable, the majority of elemental beings are using all their magic powers to make it happen. They know this period of rest is needed and are not bothered about any potential losses: since the supernatural world is busier than our visible world, they are not worried about the death or future of any single individual. From their point of view, that's a

very narrow-minded way of thinking and doesn't count. Unfortunately, there are no predictions about when the new Little Ice Age might come, so people just carry on as before and think about something else in the meantime.

Acknowledgements

The Green Ring as a concept was first mentioned in June 2007 during a Lech Zürs Tourism summer workshop. From the outset, the idea was supported by many of the local people, especially the company Skilifte Lech and the community of Lech. The project entitled "The Green Ring" was then developed further and guided by a team working in co-operation with Dr. Christian Mikunda. The artistic concept was created under the auspices of the sculptor Daniel Nikolaus Kocher and the author Daniela Egger, making it possible to experience "The Green Ring" in summer 2010 as a very special trail.

Many thanks to:

Skilifte Lech: Michael Manhart, Paul and
    Christoph Pfefferkorn
Raiffeisenbank Lech: Klaudia and Bernd Fischer
The community of Lech: Mayor Ludwig Muxel,
    hiking trails expert Stefan Burger,
    building yard manager Günter Schneider
*Representatives of the Tourism Advisory Board for
    the community of Lech:* Gitti Birk,
    Stefan Bischof, Georg Strolz, Clemens Walch
Mountain and hiking guide: Herbert Tschuggnall
And the contributing artists

Lech Zürs Tourismus GmbH:
Chairman of the Advisory Board Axel Pfefferkorn,
Director Gerhard Walter,
Project Manager Germana Nagler

Biographies of the artists:

Daniel Nikolaus Kocher

Born in Zams, Tyrol, in 1981, he trained as a sculptor in Elbigenalp and Munich and achieved a master's degree in sculpture. He has worked as a freelance artist since 2001 and has workshops in Vienna and Pitztal. He has also participated in numerous international sculpture symposia and exhibitions. In 2005, he won the Dannerpreis award for his art nouveau piece in Munich as well as outdoor installations in Imst, Basel and Umbria. In 2008, he was invited to exhibit at the Innsbruck Kunstbrücke exhibition centre as part of the RLB Art Awards.

www.daniko.at

Daniela Egger

Born in 1967 in Hohenems, she is a graduate of the Fashion Design School in Vienna. She then travelled extensively, and has been a freelance author since 1994. She has won numerous prizes and awards, including the *Graz Academy's Playwright Competition in 2000* (theatre) and the *ORF* [Austrian Broadcasting Corporation] *Prize for Film and Television Material 2002* (screenplay). She was also editor of the anthology *Austern im Schnee und andere Sommergeschichten* [Oysters in the Snow and other Summer Stories] released by Bucher Publishing House in 2008. In 2005, she co-founded and continues to be editor of the literary magazine *miromente*.

www.daniela-egger.at